The Ugly Duckling

Retold and dramatised from the
Hans Christian Andersen story as a reading play
for partners or small groups.

Ellie Hallett

Ways to read this story

This story is suitable for school and home. Some 'how to read' ideas are below.

- With a partner or small group, take it in turns to read the rows.

- Don't rush! This helps you to say each word clearly.

- Think of yourselves as actors by adding lots of facial and vocal expression. Small gaps of silence also create dramatic energy. These techniques will bring the story to life.

- If you meet a new word, try to break it down and then say it again. If you have any problems, ask your teacher or a reading buddy.

- Don't be scared of unusual words. They will become your new best friends. (New words strengthen your general knowledge and enable you to become vocabulary-rich in your day-to-day life.)

Have fun!

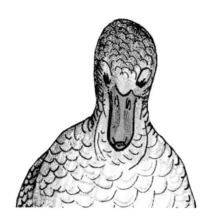

Once upon a time there was there was a mother duck whose nest was in a warm, safe spot under some large leaves that grew beside Sky Blue Lake.

It was late spring, and already the days were getting longer and warmer after the cold, dark winter.

It was a very busy time on Sky Blue Lake. Water-bird parents were busy teaching their baby birds how to swim and hunt for food.

Bees were buzzing, dragonflies were darting and birds were singing.

The mother duck was still sitting on her clutch of nine eggs, wondering if they would ever hatch.

One egg was bigger than the rest, but she sat patiently, keeping them all dry and warm.

On the day when the tadpoles started turning into frogs, there was a sound of egg-shells breaking. Only the big egg was yet to hatch.

But just as the sun rose above the horizon the next day, the big egg finally cracked open.

Out came a large baby duckling with soft grey down to join the family.

'At last! And what a handsome big baby you are!'

'But oh deary me. I wonder why you are a grey colour. All my other ducklings are fluffy yellow.'

'Well, I can't worry about things I can't change.'

So she didn't worry, and she looked proudly at all her babies.

'It is time to take you down to the pond for your first swim and show you off to all the other mother water-birds.'

So down through the water reeds they went until they came to the Sky Blue Lake.

'Stay close to me so that you don't get lost. And watch out for the geese. They often hiss and say unkind things to new babies.'

The mother duck quacked loudly, checking all the while to see that all her ducklings were following.

'First you must learn how to paddle with your webbed feet. Don't be frightened!'

To her great surprise, the grey duckling was able to swim before all the others. Off he went like a champion!

'Fancy my youngest being such a good swimmer! And to think that he only hatched out of his egg this morning.'

'He is going to make us all very proud.'

But there was trouble ahead. Other water-birds saw how different the large grey duckling was from them.

'Ha, ha, ha! What sort of ugly duckling are you?'

'Why is your neck long and skinny and your feet so, ha ha ha, so big?'

'You're not the same as us. You don't fit in here. We're going to tease you, and no one is going to like you one little bit. Ha, ha!'

'Take no notice of those unfriendly water birds, my little champion. It's not how you look but how you *are* that's important.'

But this was easier said than done.

Although the mother duck and her nine ducklings went to a sheltered spot in Sky Blue Lake, things went from bad to worse.

The geese found the grey duckling and became noisier and nastier.

Worst of all, the geese hissed and chased the grey duckling far away from his mother and brothers and sisters.

He suddenly found himself in a very strange place and a long way from his family.

Large birds flapped their wings and strutted and crowed as if they were better than everyone else.

'Welcome to your new home, Ugly Duckling. You'll never find your way back to your mother now.'

'You can join these other silly hen and rooster birds that can't fly. Let *them* put up with you. Ha, ha, ha!'

And off went the hissing geese, arguing and laughing amongst themselves as they went.

But there was no time for the grey duckling to gather his thoughts.

A large rooster with beady eyes was glaring down from his perch on top of a hen-house.

'Well, aren't you the ugliest thing in the whole wide world!'

'Have a look at this new arrival, hens, and tell me what you think of *this* odd creature!'

'K-warck, k-warck. We agree! We've never seen such ugliness in all our lives.'

'Let's peck him with our sharp beaks and chase him around the farmyard. Yuk!'

'Why doesn't anyone like me? I have feelings just like everyone else. I can't help the way I look.'

Suddenly a hunting dog began to bark.

The hunting dog was sniffing loudly with his nose to the ground. He could smell the Ugly Duckling and he was very keen to find him.

The dog had almost reached the Ugly Duckling when a human voice called out loudly.

'Here Rusty! Here, boy! Time for dinner!'

And off went the hunting dog in the opposite direction, his tail in the air and his nose sniffing for dinner smells.

'What a lucky escape *that* was. But I don't feel safe enough to stay here.'

'The world seems to be full of dangers. The sun is setting, so I need to find a safe place to sleep.'

Darkness was falling when the grey duckling came at last to an old barn.

'This looks like a warm safe place to shelter. Oh, how tired I am!'

'Coo, coo. What are you? This roost is taken, so you can't sleep up here. We pigeons are definitely not going to share.'

'I don't need a roost. I'll be happy on the floor, thank you, pigeons. I'll be so quiet you won't even know I am here.'

And the Ugly Duckling fell asleep in an instant. The pigeons thought about things for a moment, and then they also put their heads under their wings and went back to sleep.

The moon came and went, the stars shone brightly then slowly faded. The sun rose, turning the dark sky a soft shade of pink.

'Well, good morning, and what have we here!'

An old woman and a large ginger cat stood looking at the Ugly Duckling with great interest.

'Well, puss, I think we have a visitor, a very handy visitor. Yes, a very handy visitor indeed!'

'This ugly ducky creature will be just the thing to give me lovely big eggs.'

And the ginger cat swished his tail and purred loudly.

But after a few months the woman became impatient.

'Either you lay me an egg soon, duck, or off you go. You can stay for one week more, but if you can't give me eggs, you're out!'

The leaves began to turn from green to yellow. The world outside was changing.

The winds became rough and biting, pulling the leaves off the trees, leaving silvery bare branches.

'Thank goodness I've grown bigger. The trouble is, instead of being an ugly duckling, I've become an ugly duck, and there's not much joy in that!'

One cold morning a week later, the old woman had made her decision.

'That's it, duck or whatever you are! The first snowflakes are starting to fall, so it's time you left.'

'I can't afford to feed you over the winter if you give me nothing in return.'

'At least my cat keeps me warm at night and catches mice! What use is a duck that doesn't lay eggs?'

The harsh voice of the old woman made the Ugly Duck shiver.

'Why is everyone I meet so unkind? I'm no bother, but I know when I'm not wanted.'

'I need a good swim to clear my head so that I can decide what to do next.'

There was a stream nearby where the thin bare branches of the willow trees fell into the water as if they were weeping.

'There's something funny going on. The world is losing its warm colours, and even the blue water in the stream has turned into a hard, icy white.'

Suddenly there was a different sound in the crisp, cold air. It was the swishing noise of large wings slicing through the air.

The grey duck looked up to see the most wonderful sight he had ever seen in his whole life.

It was a formation of beautiful white birds flying overhead.

'I wonder what type of birds they are! How dazzling they are with their long, slender necks outstretched as they fly.'

'How wonderful it must be to look like them, and to have so many friends for company.'

'I would give anything to look like that, but I must put such ideas out of my head.'

'I need to just accept the fact that I'll be ugly and grey and have to be by myself for the rest of my life.'

Time passed.

Food was hard to find, and the stream was barely flowing.

A strange, dark and eerie stillness filled the air.

'Oh deary me! The stream has frozen over with ice. There's no food anywhere, and I feel so cold and lonely.'

The snow continued to fall and the night wind blew fiercely against the bare trees.

Eventually the Ugly Duck fell into a deep and troubled sleep.

The long dark hours closed in around him and he stayed very still.

The next day there was an excited cry of children as they came running in the pale winter sunshine.

'Hey, look at the stream! It's frozen. We'll be able to go skating this afternoon!'

'Oh no! What's this? Come over here and look what I've found! Poor thing! He's only just alive.'

'We'd better take him home straight away and put him by the fire and give him something to eat to try and save his life.'

'I wonder why he didn't fly away for the winter like the other birds.'

The children were kind and gentle, and they looked after him all through the winter.

He grew as strong and as handsome as a bird was able to grow.

Spring finally arrived. The bare silver branches of the trees burst into blossom overnight, filling the world with colour.

The willow trees sprouted new green leaves, bees hummed in the blossom trees, and the mother frogs croaked happily in quiet pools near the stream.

Water-birds returned from far away and started building nests.

The Ugly Duck stretched his wings and also felt the call of spring.

'The children have gone back to school, and in the afternoons they are busy looking after the new baby lambs. It's time for me to look after myself.'

Still believing he was ugly, he arrived where the willow tree branches stretched once again down to the water.

The stream gurgled and flowed gently in the warm sunshine.

'Oh no. I'm too late. The stream has already been taken by other birds. They will tell me not to bother them, so I will have to move on yet again!'

'Oh, deary me! They are the same beautiful birds I saw when they flew overhead in formation.'

'I'd better leave. They won't want a duck for company, and certainly not an ugly one like me.'

But instead of hissing and telling him to go away, the beautiful birds with the long necks called out to him in friendly voices.

'We haven't seen you before. Would you like to join our wedge of swans?'

'Swans? What are you talking about?'

'I used to be an ugly duckling and now I'm an ugly duck. No, I'll keep out of your way. No-one likes ugly grey.'

'What are you talking about?'

'Have a look at yourself in the stream! What do you see?'

'Oh me oh my! Is this really what I look like?'

'Am I a-a-a swan? But swans are beautiful. I've always been ugly, and because I'm ugly, no-one wants to have anything to do with me.'

'Baby swans are a soft grey colour when they hatch. As they get older, their feathers grow into pure white or glorious black, according to where they live.'

'Your egg must have somehow been put into a mother duck's nest by mistake.'

'Our mother was a swan, so she was able to protect us.'

'Your mother was a duck. Although she tried to keep you safe, she was far too small to fight those big bossy birds.'

'And at the end of summer we fly to a warm country far away. We would love you to be a part of our family.'

'It sounds wonderful! Oh, I am so happy!'

Later that day, the children who had saved the swan from the frozen stream in the cold mid-winter looked up and saw a wedge of magnificent swans flying overhead.

'Look! That's the swan we saved!'

'See how well his strong wings cut through the air and how still and steady his head is as he flies.'

'I have a family at last. And no one will ever again call me The Ugly Duckling!'